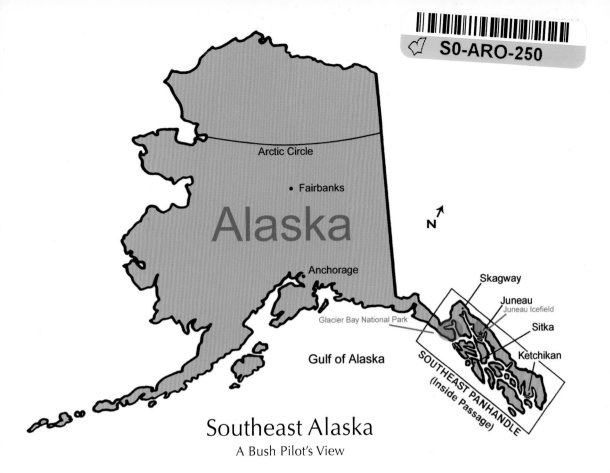

Arctic Circle

• Fairbanks

Alaska

N

Anchorage

Glacier Bay National Park

Skagway

Juneau
Juneau Icefield

Sitka

Ketchikan

Gulf of Alaska

SOUTHEAST PANHANDLE
(Inside Passage)

Southeast Alaska
A Bush Pilot's View

High Over Alaska Series, Volume One

Photography & Text
Buddy Ferguson

Published by
CRF Images

Printed in the U.S.A.
Ross Printing Company
Spokane, Washington

Inquiries
www.crfimages.com

ISBN 0-9740066-0-2

Acknowledgement

For me, aerial photography works best as a solitary experience. Ultimately, however, my goal is to share the unique perspective flight offers with other people. To complete this project required the contribution of numerous persons. For all of you who commented, advised, challenged and remained patient throughout the evolution of this aerial collection - THANK YOU!

Especially,

Mary Lou

Buddy Ferguson

Notes and References:

Community population data from Alaska Department of Community and Economic Development 2002 demographics.

Orth, Donald. *Dictionary of Alaska Place Names*. United States Government Printing Office, Reprinted 1971. United States Department of Interior. Geological Survey Professional Paper 567.

◆ Image available as Giclee Print

For the past two decades, I have been fortunate to routinely explore some of earth's most spectacular geography and wilderness from the pilot's seat of numerous small airplanes.

This collection of aerial prints offers a glimpse of the dynamic perspective of flight in Southeast Alaska.

Buddy Ferguson
pilot & photographer

Cover photo: High over the Mendenhall Glacier. Juneau, Alaska

Juneau Icefield. Termination dust, the first snow on the mountains in the fall, had long since turned to snow accumulation at the higher elevations. I had spent the day flying floatplane charters, but the late afternoon light was simply superb, so I grabbed my camera bag and was airborne again. Without the daytime position-reporting chatter over the radio, I eased into an uninterrupted world. As the long-defined shadows on the snow slowly faded, I realized my camera was still snugly packed away. This view looking northward from over the Taku Towers was the only photo I shot that October evening.

October Sunset Over The Juneau Icefield

Juneau Icefield. After finishing a summer-flying season based north of the Arctic Circle in Bettles, I was returning home to Juneau. The day was rather hazy, so shooting aerial photos on the last leg of the flight appeared unlikely. As I neared Berners Bay, 50 miles northwest of downtown Juneau, the air sharpened under scattered cirrus clouds. Maneuvering for this photo and several other shots between the Gilkey River and upper Eagle Glacier made this homecoming rather memorable.

Glacial Icefall

Juneau Icefield. Several years ago while flying for Ward Air, Dennis Lozier, Arne Johnson and I had some down time between charter flights. Having near-perfect light and unscheduled airplanes was too good to be true, so we launched. Dennis flew the camera plane, a Cessna 185, while Arne piloted the DeHavilland Beaver floatplane shown opposite. Getting this shot required the pilots to match airspeeds and then maneuver into formation, all while staying vigilant for other air traffic and some very imposing terrain. This image was used in the company's 2001 calendar.

DeHavilland Beaver Floatplane

Juneau Icefield. South of the U.S. - Canadian border, five distinct glaciers radiate off the ice field and empty meltwater into the Taku River valley. Many Alaska rivers become braided complexes of sandbars and shallow channels as glacial silt accumulates. The Norris and Taku glaciers (above) are the first two rivers of ice encountered when you fly northbound up the Taku River. The first signs of fall color along the rebounding "Grizzly Bar" (opposite) signal that the frenetic pace of summer flying is winding down.

Norris Glacier and The Grizzly Bar

Juneau Icefield. The East Twin Glacier along the Taku River epitomizes Southeast Alaska glaciers. An ice fall origin, serpentine flow, moraines and a fractured vertical face terminating in a recessional lake - all these elements are compressed into a short horizontal run which is clearly visible from a single aerial viewpoint. For glacier flightseeing, I prefer cloudy skies. On these overcast days the blue saturation in the dense glacial ice is enhanced and the air is generally smoother too.

East Twin Glacier

Juneau Icefield. I never tire of viewing the many shapes, colors and eroded formations associated with glaciers. As temperatures warm during the summer months, water from snowmelt often collects in ice field depressions and crevasses. These pools range in color from emerald green to cobalt blue. After watching this pool develop for over a month, I finally photographed it one late afternoon in August. Visible on the hillside are two small avalanches.

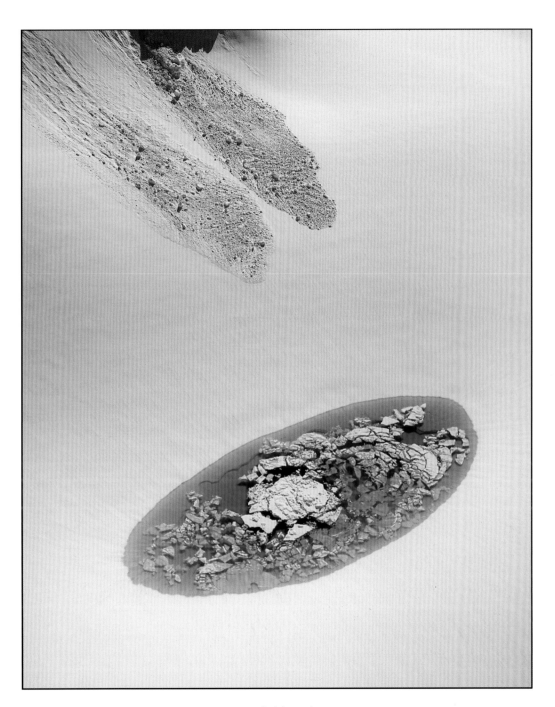

Icefield Pool ◆

Juneau Icefield. Smooth air is a definite prerequisite for my style of oblique aerial photography. During the shooting process, my hands must be free of the aircraft controls to operate the camera. Getting this shot of the Antler Glacier was quite a challenge due to the proximity of the mountains. After several practice runs, I worked out a flight sequence that gave me the moments needed to take this photograph. A decade ago, this glacier flowed over the vertical rock wall to the valley floor several thousand feet below.

Blue Cascade

Juneau Icefield. Each Alaska mountain range is visually unique. Near-vertical relief characterizes the Coast Mountains of Southeast. These peaks rise from sea level and many are snow and ice-capped year around. This granite spire behind the Eagle Glacier shows the formidability of these mountains. Strong low-pressure weather systems spinning onshore from the Gulf of Alaska are forced to unload their moisture when colliding with this terrain. The Coast Mountains may not have the tallest peaks in the state, but their drama is not easily surpassed.

The Coast Mountains

Juneau Icefield. When I moved to Juneau in 1972, the face of the Mendenhall Glacier extended forward and nearly covered the peninsula of polished rock protruding from the left. Scientists say that an average cooling of our climate by even two degrees could easily reverse the current state of glacial recession. Advancing or receding, such a readily viewable natural wonder makes Juneau a unique place to live or visit.

Mendenhall Glacier

Glacier Bay. The smallest of the three ice fields in Southeast Alaska was named after John G. Brady, a missionary who served as territorial governor of Alaska from 1897-1909. The Fairweather Range, composed of peaks rising to 15,000 feet, cast sunset shadows on this field of snow and ice. Diminishing daylight made this the last picture of a four-hour photo mission along the Gulf of Alaska coastline between Cape Spencer and the Alsek River.

Brady Icefield

Glacier Bay. I shot this image of the Johns Hopkins Glacier from its upper amphitheater near Mount Crillon. On nice weather days, this route is a great aerial shortcut through the Fairweather Range to the gulf coast. About 100 years ago this glacier joined with the Grand Pacific ten miles down the inlet and created a single ice sheet which filled much of Glacier Bay's west arm. University professor Henry F. Reid named this glacier in 1893 after his sponsoring institution.

Johns Hopkins Glacier

Glacier Bay. Nearly all of my aerial photo excursions are done solo. I remember this day rather well because a special friend was along for the trip. After flying around Glacier Bay's west arm, we crossed the Grand Pacific and Melbern glaciers into the Tatshenshini and Alsek river drainages. Following these braided rivers brought us to the Gulf of Alaska at Dry Bay where we headed west along the surf line into Yakutat. On the return flight to Juneau, I shot this image of the Grand Plateau. Four major glacial tributaries flow out of the Fairweather Range to create this ice sheet. As these branches join, eroded debris piles together and is carried along as medial moraines.

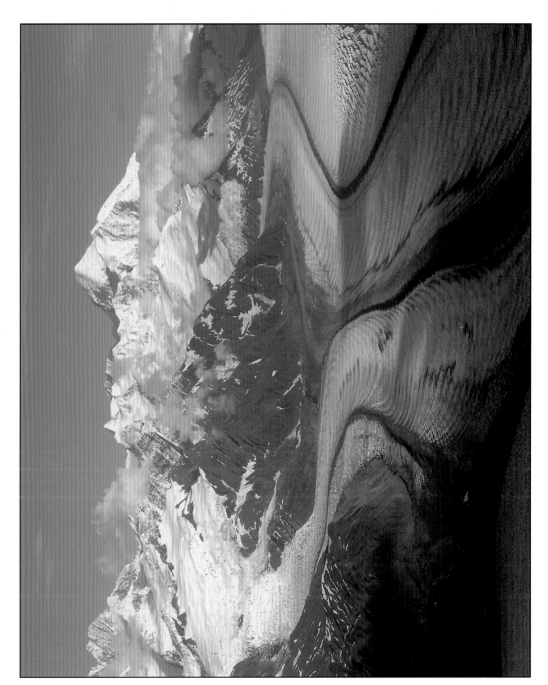

Mount Fairweather and Grand Plateau Glacier

Glacier Bay. Stratified layers, comparable to growth rings in a tree, are revealed at the terminal face of the Grand Plateau Glacier. The textures and colors of these powerful earth-movers make them fascinating photo subjects. Cold air descends, resulting in breezy conditions in the vicinity of a glacier's terminus. Even on warm days, a jacket is often necessary near these rivers of ice.

Glacial Stratiform

Glacier Bay. Most of Southeast Alaska is covered by temperate rain forest, predominately of Sitka spruce and Western hemlock. A striking contrast to this lush green landscape can be found sixty miles up Glacier Bay at the head of Tarr Inlet. Here glacier scoured mountainsides are just beginning to show signs of vegetation. Cruise ships visiting this national park often pause at the Margerie and Grand Pacific tidewater glaciers. Ice calving from the terminal faces of these glaciers is an awesome event all park visitors hope to experience. By normal standards this September afternoon was an exceptionally clear day. Often atmospheric particulates like smoke, pollen, dust, and salt spray are present and soften the clarity of aerial photos.

Margerie Glacier

Glacier Bay. One Easter Sunday I flew my airplane from Fairbanks to Juneau. The entire state was dominated by high pressure and the surface winds were almost nil. After refueling in Northway, I crossed the Wrangell-St. Elias Mountains, followed the Bagley Icefield to Icy Bay and then descended into Yakutat for my final fuel stop. I was an hour from Juneau when I saw these fascinating snowdrifts on the Rendu Glacier. After shooting a couple rolls of film, I turned on a direct course for Juneau so I would not be late for dinner.

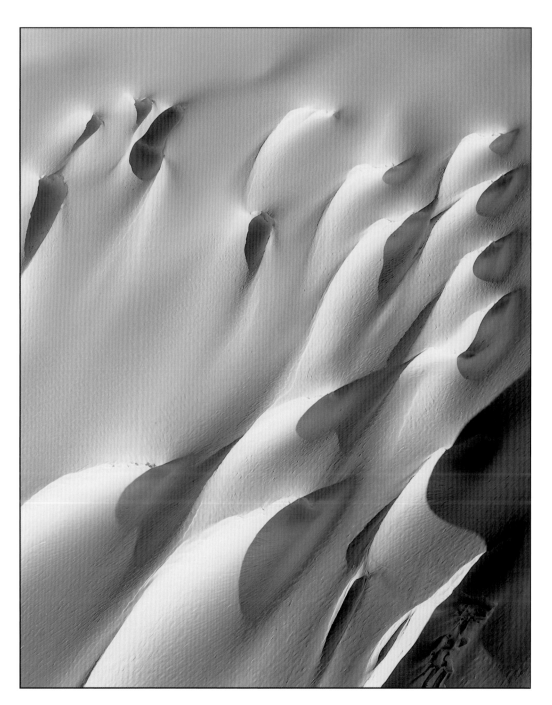

Snow Sculpture ◆

Glacier Bay. The Casement is a great example of a glacier withdrawn from tidewater. Meltwater now flows as a small braided river into Adams Inlet which was completely filled with ice one hundred years ago. The rapid changes in Glacier Bay are particulary evident in the east arm. Near the terminal face of many glaciers, the landscape appears very desert-like. For pilots, the Casement is an airway into and out of this national park from northern Lynn Canal. Except for the outer coast, this region of Glacier Bay is my favorite to photograph.

Casement Glacier - Adams Inlet

Ketchikan, Alaska. (pop. 14,070) Although this town has a reputation for having a wet climate, Ketchikan really shines when the clouds part. In terms of distance, most Southeast communites are not far from each other. Without connecting roads, however, Panhandle towns often feel worlds apart. Being an air taxi pilot has enabled me to visit many of these communities over the years. From the airstrips to the seaplane docks, I have discovered Southeast Alaskans to be both incredibly hospitable and remarkably generous neighbors.

Ketchikan, Alaska

Sitka, Alaska. (pop. 8,894)   Several years ago I had the opportunity to fly a U.S. Forest Service contract in Sitka. I really enjoyed becoming better acquainted with this former capital of Russian Alaska. Being seaside is a way of life in Southeast. On Sitka Sound, ocean swells pulse along with the changing tides. Walking the harbor docks, strolling along Katlian Street, tasting the salt air and listening to an orchestra of maritime sounds are some of my fondest memories of Sitka.

Sitka, Alaska

Juneau, Alaska. (pop. 30,981) Describing this town in words is as difficult as it is to portray in a single photograph. In Alaska's capital city you seldom hear argument over quality of life. Surrounded by stunning geography, Juneau, like most Southeast communities, seamlessly blends with wilderness. The image of Juneau International Airport (opposite) was shot one late afternoon in October from over Auke Bay looking east down Gastineau Channel. Juneau's downtown (above), a mixture of government, business and residential buildings, rests at the base of Mount Juneau and Mount Roberts.

Juneau, Alaska ◆

Skagway, Alaska. (pop. 841) Over the last two decades, I have flown into and out of Skagway through the narrow Taiya Inlet hundreds of times. To capture the context of a town through an oblique aerial photograph can be a compositional challenge, especially here in Southeast Alaska. Of all my images of Skagway, this easterly looking view from across the inlet best shows the stunning, near-vertical backdrop to this seasonal boomtown. Behind these coastal peaks, glaciated valleys interconnect with the Juneau Icefield. One of Skagway's unique features is a highway to Canada and Alaska's interior, which makes this town a vital port in the region.

Skagway, Alaska

Sunsets are a great visual metaphor for a closing. This image of Lynn Canal looks northwest towards Haines and Skagway from about eight miles west of the Juneau Airport. Some people take short car drives to relax; I often jump into my airplane for the same reason, but never without a camera on board. Even though this flight lasted only twenty minutes, I was fortunate to capture the tranquil mood on film.

Lynn Canal Sunset

This 1954 Cessna 170B is my principal aerial photography platform. I am often asked, "How can you fly **and** take pictures?" Because of the viewing and mobility restrictions while seated in a small airplane, photo composition essentially becomes an exercise in aircraft positioning. For me, flying the airplane so that I can capture an image on film is much easier than trying to communicate with another pilot about where to maneuver the aircraft.

The photographs in this collection were all shot using a Mamiya 6x7 medium format camera. I generally use a 150mm lens, a 73mm lens equivalent in 35mm format. The original film images were then scanned for press reproduction.

After two decades of professional flying in Alaska, I am still hooked on her awesome beauty. With ever-changing light this incredible geography never becomes visually boring. With limited road access, especially here in Southeast, the best way to put this magnificence into context is from the air. I am delighted to share my passion for aerial photography with you by way of this presentation.

Southeast Alaska Totem

Glacial Snow Sculpture

Southeast Alaska Totem, Kake, Alaska

Postage

"Eye to Eye" 16" x 20" Giclee Print ©Buddy Ferguson

Snowdrifts on the Rendu Glacier
Glacier Bay National Park

Postage

"Snow Sculpture" 16" x 20" Giclee Print ©Buddy Ferguson